OUR UNIVERSE

HIMANSHU KUMAR

© Himanshu Kumar 2023

All rights reserved

All rights reserved by author. No part of this publication may be reproduced, stored in a retrieval system or transmitted in any form or by any means, electronic, mechanical, photocopying, recording or otherwise, without the prior permission of the author.

Although every precaution has been taken to verify the accuracy of the information contained herein, the author and publisher assume no responsibility for any errors or omissions. No liability is assumed for damages that may result from the use of information contained within.

First Published in May 2023

ISBN: 978-93-5741-711-2

BLUEROSE PUBLISHERS

www.BlueRoseONE.com

info@bluerosepublishers.com

+91 8882 898 898

Cover Design:

Yash

Typographic Design:

Hemlata

Distributed by: BlueRose, Amazon, Flipkart

Contents

Chapter 1: The Sun 1

Chapter 2: The Mercury 12

Chapter 3: The Venus 18

Chapter 4: The Earth 29

Chapter 5: The Mars 36

Chapter 6: The Jupiter 43

Chapter 7: The Saturn 51

Chapter 8: The Uranus 57

Chapter 9: The Neptune 64

Chapter 1

The Sun

Overview

Our Sun is a 4.5 billion-year-old star – a hot glowing ball of hydrogen and helium at the center of our solar system. The Sun is about 93 million miles (150 million kilometers) from Earth, and without its energy, life as we know it could not exist here on our home planet. The Sun is the largest object in our solar system. The Sun's volume would need 1.3 million Earths to fill it. Its gravity holds the solar system together, keeping everything from the biggest planets to the smallest bits of debris in orbit around it. The hottest part of the Sun is its core, where temperatures top 27 million degrees Fahrenheit (15 million degrees Celsius). The Sun's activity, from its powerful eruptions to the steady stream of charged particles it sends out, influences the nature of space throughout the solar system. NASA and other international space agencies monitor the Sun 24/7 with a fleet of spacecraft, studying everything from its atmosphere to its surface, and even peering inside the Sun using special instruments. Sun-exploring spacecraft include Parker Solar Probe, Solar Orbiter, SOHO, ACE, IRIS, WIND, Hinode, Solar Dynamics Observatory, and STEREO.

In Depth

The Sun is a 4.5 billion-year-old yellow dwarf star – a hot glowing ball of hydrogen and helium – at the center of our solar system. It's about 93 million miles (150 million kilometers) from Earth and it's our solar system's only star. Without the Sun's energy, life as we know it could not exist on our home planet.

From our vantage point on Earth, the Sun may appear like an unchanging source of light and heat in the sky. But the Sun is a dynamic star, constantly changing and sending energy out into space. The science of studying the Sun and its influence throughout the solar system is called heliophysics.

The Sun Is the largest object in our solar system. Its diameter is about 865,000 miles (1.4 million kilometers). Its gravity holds the solar system together, keeping everything from the biggest planets to the smallest bits of debris in orbit around it.

Even though the Sun is the center of our solar system and essential to our survival, it's only an average star in terms of its size. Stars up to 100 times larger have been found. And many solar systems have more than one star. By studying our Sun, scientists can better understand the workings of distant stars.

The hottest part of the Sun is its core, where temperatures top 27 million °F (15 million °C). The part of the Sun we call its surface – the photosphere – is a relatively cool 10,000 °F (5,500 °C). In one of the Sun's biggest mysteries, the Sun's outer atmosphere, the corona, gets hotter the farther it stretches from the surface. The corona reaches up to 3.5

million F (2 million C) – much, much hotter than the photosphere.

Namesake

The Sun has been called by many names. The Latin word for Sun is "sol," which is the main adjective for all things Sun-related: solar. Helios, the Sun god in ancient Greek mythology, lends his name to many Sun-related terms as well, such as heliosphere and helioseismology.

Potential for Life

The Sun could not harbor life as we know it because of its extreme temperatures and radiation. Yet life on Earth is only possible because of the Sun's light and energy.

Size and Distance

Our Sun is a medium-sized star with a radius of about 435,000 miles (700,000 kilometers). Many stars are much larger – but the Sun is far more massive than our home planet: it would take more than 330,000 Earths to match the mass of the Sun, and it would take 1.3 million Earths to fill the Sun's volume.

The Sun Is about 93 million miles (150 million kilometers) from Earth. Its nearest stellar neighbor is the Alpha Centauri triple star system: red dwarf star Proxima Centauri is 4.24 light-years away, and Alpha Centauri A and B – two sunlike stars orbiting each other – are 4.37 light-years away. A light-year is the distance light travels in one year, which equals about 6 trillion miles (9.5 trillion kilometers).

Orbit and Rotation

The Sun is located in the Milky Way galaxy in a spiral arm called the Orion Spur that extends outward from the Sagittarius arm. The Sun orbits the center of the Milky Way, bringing with it the planets, asteroids, comets, and other objects in our solar system. Our solar system is moving with an average velocity of 450,000 miles per hour (720,000 kilometers per hour). But even at this speed, it takes about 230 million years for the Sun to make one complete trip around the Milky Way.

The Sun rotates on Its axis as it revolves around the galaxy. Its spin has a tilt of 7.25 degrees with respect to the plane of the planets' orbits. Since the Sun is not solid, different parts rotate at different rates. At the equator, the Sun spins around once about every 25 Earth days, but at its poles, the Sun rotates once on its axis every 36 Earth days.

Moons

As a star, the Sun doesn't have any moons, but the planets and their moons orbit the Sun.

Rings

The Sun would have been surrounded by a disk of gas and dust early in its history when the solar system was first forming, about 4.6 billion years ago. Some of that dust is still around today, in several dust rings that circle the Sun. They trace the orbits of planets, whose gravity tugs dust into place around the Sun.

Formation

The Sun formed about 4.6 billion years ago in a giant, spinning cloud of gas and dust called the solar nebula. As the nebula collapsed under its own gravity, it spun faster and flattened into a disk. Most of the nebula's material was pulled toward the center to form our Sun, which accounts for 99.8% of our solar system's mass. Much of the remaining material formed the planets and other objects that now orbit the Sun. (The rest of the leftover gas and dust was blown away by the young Sun's early solar wind.)

Like all stars, our Sun will eventually run out of energy. When it starts to die, the Sun will expand into a red giant star, becoming so large that it will engulf Mercury and Venus, and possibly Earth as well. Scientists predict the Sun is a little less than halfway through its lifetime and will last another 5 billion years or so before it becomes a white dwarf.

Structure

The Sun is a huge ball of hydrogen and helium held together by its own gravity.

The Sun has several regions. The interior regions include the core, the radiative zone, and the convection zone. Moving outward – the visible surface or photosphere is next, then the chromosphere, followed by the transition zone, and then the corona – the Sun's expansive outer atmosphere.

Once material leaves the corona at supersonic speeds, it becomes the solar wind, which forms a huge magnetic "bubble" around the Sun, called the heliosphere. The heliosphere extends beyond the orbit of the planets in our solar system. Thus, Earth exists inside the Sun's atmosphere. Outside the heliosphere is interstellar space.

The core is the hottest part of the Sun. Nuclear reactions here – where hydrogen is fused to form helium – power the Sun's heat and light. Temperatures top 27 million F (15 million °C) and it's about 86,000 miles (138,000 kilometers) thick. The density of the Sun's core is about 150 grams per cubic centimeter (g/cm^3). That is approximately 8 times the density of gold (19.3 g/cm^3) or 13 times the density of lead (11.3 g/cm^3).

Energy from the core is carried outward by radiation. This radiation bounces around the radiative zone, taking about 170,000 years to get from the core to the top of the convection zone. Moving outward, in the convection zone, the temperature drops below 3.5 million °F (2 million °C). Here, large bubbles of hot plasma (a soup of ionized atoms) move upward toward the photosphere, which is the layer we think of as the Sun's surface.

Surface

The Sun doesn't have a solid surface like Earth and the other rocky planets and moons. The part of the Sun commonly called its surface is the photosphere. The word photosphere means "light sphere" – which is apt because this is the layer that emits the most visible light. It's what we see from Earth with our eyes. (Hopefully, it goes without saying – but never look directly at the Sun without protecting your eyes.)

Although we call it the surface, the photosphere is actually the first layer of the solar atmosphere. It's about 250 miles thick, with temperatures reaching about 10,000 degrees Fahrenheit (5,500 degrees Celsius). That's much cooler than the blazing core, but it's still hot enough to make carbon - like diamonds and graphite - not just melt, but boil. Most of the Sun's radiation escapes outward from the photosphere into space.

Atmosphere

Above the photosphere is the chromosphere, the transition zone, and the corona. Not all scientists refer to the transition zone as its own region - it is simply the thin layer where the chromosphere rapidly heats and becomes the corona. The photosphere, chromosphere, and corona are all part of the Sun's atmosphere. (The corona is sometimes casually referred to as "the Sun's atmosphere," but it is actually the Sun's upper atmosphere.)

The Sun's atmosphere is where we see features such as sunspots, coronal holes, and solar flares.Key Sun Features

Spicules

At any given moment, as many as 10 million wild jets of solar material burst up from the Sun's surface. Known as spicules, these grass-like tendrils of plasma erupt as fast as 60 miles per second (100 kilometers per second) and can reach lengths of 6,000 miles (9,700 kilometers) before collapsing. Credit: NASA's Goddard Space Flight Center

Visible light from these top regions of the Sun is usually too weak to be seen against the brighter photosphere, but during total solar eclipses, when the Moon covers the photosphere, the chromosphere looks like a fine, red rim around the Sun, while the corona forms a beautiful white crown ("corona" means crown in Latin and Spanish) with plasma streamers narrowing outward, forming shapes that look like flower petals.

In one of the Sun's biggest mysteries, the corona is much hotter than the layers immediately below it. (Imagine walking away from a bonfire only to get warmer.) The source of coronal heating is a major unsolved puzzle in the study of the Sun.

Magnetosphere

The Sun generates magnetic fields that extend out into space to form the interplanetary magnetic field – the magnetic field that pervades our solar system. The field is carried through the solar system by the solar wind – a stream of electrically charged gas blowing outward from the Sun in all directions. The vast bubble of space dominated by the Sun's magnetic field is called the heliosphere. Since the Sun rotates, the magnetic field spins out into a large rotating spiral, known as the Parker spiral. This spiral has a shape something like the pattern of water from a rotating garden sprinkler.

The Sun doesn't behave the same way all the time. It goes through phases of high and low activity, which make up the solar cycle. Approximately every 11 years, the Sun's geographic poles change their magnetic polarity – that is, the north and south magnetic poles swap. During this cycle, the Sun's photosphere, chromosphere, and corona change from quiet and calm to violently active.

The height of the Sun's activity cycle, known as solar maximum, is a time of greatly increased solar storm activity.

Sunspots, eruptions called solar flares, and coronal mass ejections are common at solar maximum. The latest solar cycle - Solar Cycle 25 - started in December 2019 when solar minimum occurred, according to the Solar Cycle 25 Prediction Panel, an international group of experts co-sponsored by NASA and NOAA. Scientists now expect the Sun's activity to ramp up toward the next predicted maximum in July 2025.

Solar activity can release huge amounts of energy and particles, some of which impact us here on Earth. Much like weather on Earth, conditions in space - known as space weather - are always changing with the Sun's activity. "Space weather" can interfere with satellites, GPS, and radio communications. It also can cripple power grids, and corrode pipelines that carry oil and gas.

The strongest geomagnetic storm on record is the Carrington Event, named for British astronomer Richard Carrington who observed the Sept. 1, 1859, solar flare that triggered the event. Telegraph systems worldwide went haywire. Spark discharges shocked telegraph operators and set their telegraph paper on fire. Just before dawn the next day, skies all over Earth erupted in red, green, and purple auroras - the result of energy and particles from the Sun interacting with Earth's atmosphere. Reportedly, the auroras were so brilliant that newspapers could be read as easily as in daylight. The auroras, or Northern Lights, were visible as far south as Cuba, the Bahamas, Jamaica, El Salvador, and Hawaii.

Another solar flare on March 13, 1989, caused geomagnetic storms that disrupted electric power transmission from the Hydro Québec generating station in Canada, plunging 6 million people into darkness for 9 hours. The 1989 flare also caused power surges that melted power transformers in New Jersey.

In December 2005, X-rays from a solar storm disrupted satellite-to-ground communications and Global Positioning System (GPS) navigation signals for about 10 minutes.

NOAA's Space Weather Prediction Center monitors active regions on the Sun and issues watches, warnings, and alerts for hazardous space weather events.

Reference Guide
Solar System Sizes and Distances

Distance from the Sun to planets in astronomical units (au):

Planet	Distance from Sun (au)
Mercury	0.39
Venus	0.72
Earth	1
Mars	1.52
Jupiter	5.2
Saturn	9.54
Uranus	19.2
Neptune	30.06

Diameter of planets and their distance from the Sun in kilometers (km):

Planet	Diameter (km)	Distance from Sun (km)
Sun	1,391,400	-
Mercury	4,879	57,900,000
Venus	12,104	108,200,000
Earth	12,756	149,600,000
Mars	6,792	227,900,000
Jupiter	142,984	778,600,000
Saturn	120,536	1,433,500,000
Uranus	51,118	2,872,500,000
Neptune	49,528	4,495,100,000

Chapter 2.

The Mercury

Overview

The smallest planet in our solar system and nearest to the Sun, Mercury is only slightly larger than Earth's Moon.From the surface of Mercury, the Sun would appear more than three times as large as it does when viewed from Earth, and the sunlight would be as much as seven times brighter. Despite its proximity to the Sun, Mercury is not the hottest planet in our solar system – that title belongs to nearby Venus, thanks to its dense atmosphere.

Because of Mercury's elliptical – egg-shaped – orbit, and sluggish rotation, the Sun appears to rise briefly, set, and rise again from some parts of the planet's surface. The same thing happens in reverse at sunset.

In Depth

The smallest planet in our solar system and nearest to the Sun, Mercury is only slightly larger than Earth's Moon. From the surface of Mercury, the Sun would appear more than three times as large as it does when viewed from Earth, and the sunlight would be as much as seven times brighter.

Mercury's surface temperatures are both extremely hot and cold. Because the planet is so close to the Sun, day temperatures can reach highs of 800°F (430°C). Without an atmosphere to retain that heat at night, temperatures can dip as low as -290°F (-180°C).

Despite its proximity to the Sun, Mercury is not the hottest planet in our solar system – that title belongs to nearby Venus, thanks to its dense atmosphere. But Mercury is the fastest planet, zipping around the Sun every 88 Earth days.

Namesake

Mercury is appropriately named for the swiftest of the ancient Roman gods.

Potential for Life

Mercury's environment is not conducive to life as we know it. The temperatures and solar radiation that characterize this planet are most likely too extreme for organisms to adapt to.

Size and Distance

With a radius of 1,516 miles (2,440 kilometers), Mercury is a little more than 1/3 the width of Earth. If Earth were the size of a nickel, Mercury would be about as big as a blueberry.

From an average distance of 36 million miles (58 million kilometers), Mercury is 0.4 astronomical units away from the Sun. One astronomical unit (abbreviated as AU), is the distance from the Sun to Earth. From this distance, it takes sunlight 3.2 minutes to travel from the Sun to Mercury

Orbit and Rotation

Mercury's highly eccentric, egg-shaped orbit takes the planet as close as 29 million miles (47 million kilometers) and as far as 43 million miles (70 million kilometers) from the Sun. It speeds around the Sun every 88 days, traveling through space at nearly 29 miles (47 kilometers) per second, faster than any other planet.

Mercury spins slowly on its axis and completes one rotation every 59 Earth days. But when Mercury is moving fastest in its elliptical orbit around the Sun (and it is closest to the Sun), each rotation is not accompanied by sunrise and sunset like it is on most other planets. The morning Sun appears to rise briefly, set, and rise again from some parts of the planet's surface. The same thing happens in reverse at sunset for other parts of the surface. One Mercury solar day (one full day-night cycle) equals 176 Earth days – just over two years on Mercury.

Mercury's axis of rotation is tilted just 2 degrees with respect to the plane of its orbit around the Sun. That means it spins nearly perfectly upright and so does not experience seasons as many other planets do.

Moons

Mercury doesn't have moons.

Rings

Mercury doesn't have rings.

Formation

Mercury formed about 4.5 billion years ago when gravity pulled swirling gas and dust together to form this small planet nearest the Sun. Like its fellow terrestrial planets, Mercury has a central core, a rocky mantle, and a solid crust.

Structure

Mercury is the second densest planet, after Earth. It has a large metallic core with a radius of about 1,289 miles (2,074 kilometers), about 85 percent of the planet's radius. There is evidence that it is partly molten or liquid. Mercury's outer shell, comparable to Earth's outer shell (called the mantle and crust), is only about 400 kilometers (250 miles) thick.

Surface

Mercury's surface resembles that of Earth's Moon, scarred by many impact craters resulting from collisions with meteoroids and comets. Craters and features on Mercury are named after famous deceased artists, musicians, or authors, including children's author Dr. Seuss and dance pioneer Alvin Ailey.

Very large impact basins, including Caloris (960 miles or 1,550 kilometers in diameter) and Rachmaninoff (190 miles, or 306 kilometers in diameter), were created by asteroid impacts on the planet's surface early in the solar system's history. While there are large areas of smooth terrain, there are also cliffs, some hundreds of miles long and soaring up to a mile high. They rose as the planet's interior cooled and contracted over the billions of years since Mercury formed.

Most of Mercury's surface would appear greyish-brown to the human eye. The bright streaks are called "crater rays.They are formed when an asteroid or comet strikes the surface. The tremendous amount of energy that is released in such an impact digs a big hole in the ground, and also crushes a huge amount of rock under the point of impact. Some of this crushed material is thrown far from the crater and then falls to the surface, forming the rays. Fine particles of crushed rock are more reflective than large pieces, so the rays look brighter. The space environment – dust impacts and solar-wind particles – causes the rays to darken with time.

Temperatures on Mercury are extreme. During the day, temperatures on the surface can reach 800 degrees Fahrenheit (430 degrees Celsius). Because the planet has no atmosphere to retain that heat, nighttime temperatures on the surface can drop to minus 290 degrees Fahrenheit (minus 180 degrees Celsius).

Mercury may have water ice at its north and south poles inside deep craters, but only in regions in permanent shadows. In those shadows, it could be cold enough to preserve water ice despite the high temperatures on sunlit parts of the planet.

Atmosphere

Instead of an atmosphere, Mercury possesses a thin exosphere made up of atoms blasted off the surface by the solar wind and striking meteoroids. Mercury's exosphere is composed mostly of oxygen, sodium, hydrogen, helium, and potassium.

Magnetosphere

Mercury's magnetic field is offset relative to the planet's equator. Though Mercury's magnetic field at the surface has just 1% the strength of Earth's, it interacts with the magnetic field of the solar wind to sometimes create intense magnetic tornadoes that funnel the fast, hot solar wind plasma down to the surface of the planet. When the ions strike the surface, they knock off neutrally charged atoms and send them on a loop high into the sky.

Chapter 3

The Venus

Overview

Venus is the second planet from the Sun and is Earth's closest planetary neighbor. It's one of the four inner, terrestrial (or rocky) planets, and it's often called Earth's twin because it's similar in size and density. These are not identical twins, however – there are radical differences between the two worlds. Venus has a thick, toxic atmosphere filled with carbon dioxide and it's perpetually shrouded in thick, yellowish clouds of sulfuric acid that trap heat, causing a runaway greenhouse effect. It's the hottest planet in our solar system, even though Mercury is closer to the Sun. Surface temperatures on Venus are about 900 degrees Fahrenheit (475 degrees Celsius) – hot enough to melt lead. The surface is a rusty color and it's peppered with intensely crunched mountains and thousands of large volcanoes. Scientists think it's possible some volcanoes are still active.

Venus has crushing air pressure at its surface – more than 90 times that of Earth – similar to the pressure you'd encounter a mile below the ocean on Earth.

Another big difference from Earth – Venus rotates on its axis backward, compared to most of the other planets in the solar system. This means that, on Venus, the Sun rises in the west and sets in the east, opposite to what we experience on Earth.

(It's not the only planet in our solar system with such an oddball rotation – Uranus spins on its side.)

Venus was the first planet to be explored by a spacecraft – NASA's Mariner 2 successfully flew by and scanned the cloud-covered world on Dec. 14, 1962. Since then, numerous spacecraft from the U.S. and other space agencies have explored Venus, including NASA's Magellan, which mapped the planet's surface with radar. Soviet spacecraft made the most successful landings on the surface of Venus to date, but they didn't survive long due to the extreme heat and crushing pressure. An American probe, one of NASA's Pioneer Venus Multiprobes, survived for about an hour after impacting the surface in 1978.

More recent Venus missions include ESA's Venus Express (which orbited from 2006 until 2016) and Japan's Akatsuki Venus Climate Orbiter (orbiting since 2016).

NASA's Parker Solar Probe has made multiple flybys of Venus. On Feb. 9, 2022, NASA announced the spacecraft had captured its first visible light images of the surface of Venus from space during its February 2021 flyby.

In June 2021, three new missions to Venus were announced. NASA announced two new missions, and ESA announced one:

VERITAS: NASA's VERITAS, or Venus Emissivity, Radio Science, InSAR, Topography, and Spectroscopy, will be the first NASA spacecraft to explore Venus since the 1990s. The spacecraft will launch no earlier than December 2027. It will orbit Venus, gathering data to reveal how the paths of Venus and Earth diverged, and how Venus lost its potential to be a habitable world.

DAVINCI: NASA's DAVINCI mission will launch in the late 2020s. After exploring the top of Venus's atmosphere, DAVINCI will drop a probe to the surface. On its hour-long descent, the probe will take thousands of measurements and snap up-close images of the surface. The probe may not survive the landing, but if it does, it could provide several minutes of bonus science.

EnVision: ESA has selected EnVision to make detailed observations of Venus. As a key partner in the mission, NASA is providing the Synthetic Aperture Radar, called VenSAR, to make high-resolution measurements of the planet's surface features.

In Depth

It's a cloud-swaddled planet named for a love goddess, often called Earth's twin. But pull up a bit closer, and Venus turns hellish. Our nearest planetary neighbor, the second planet from the Sun, has a surface hot enough to melt lead. The atmosphere is so thick that, from the surface, the Sun is just a smear of light.

In some ways it is more an opposite of Earth than a twin: Venus spins backward, has a day longer than its year, and lacks any semblance of seasons. It might once have been a habitable ocean world, like Earth, but that was at least a billion years ago. A runaway greenhouse effect turned all surface water into vapor, which then leaked slowly into space. The present-day surface of volcanic rock is blasted by high temperatures and pressures. Asked if the surface of Venus is likely to be life-bearing today, we can give a quick answer: a hard "no."

Further, Venus may hold lessons about what it takes for life to get its start -- on Earth, in our solar system, or across the galaxy. The ingredients are all there, or at least, they used to be. By studying why our neighbor world went in such a different direction with regard to habitability, we could find out what could make other worlds right. And while it might sound absurd, we can't rule out life on Venus entirely. Temperature, air pressure, and chemistry are much more congenial up high, in those thick, yellow clouds.

Namesake

The ancient Romans could easily see seven bright objects in the sky: the Sun, the Moon, and the five brightest planets (Mercury, Venus, Mars, Jupiter, and Saturn). They named the objects after their most important gods. Venus, the third brightest object after the Sun and Moon, was named after the Roman goddess of love and beauty. It's the only planet named after a female god.

Potential for Life

Thirty miles up (about 50 kilometers), temperatures range from 86 to 158 Fahrenheit (30 to 70 Celsius), a range that, even at its higher-end, could accommodate Earthly life, such as "extremophile" microbes. And atmospheric pressure at that height is similar to what we find on Earth's surface.

At the tops of Venus' clouds, whipped around the planet by winds measured as high as 224 miles (360 kilometers) per hour, we find another transformation. Persistent, dark streaks appear. Scientists are so far unable to explain why these streaks remain stubbornly intact, even amid hurricane-force winds. They also have the odd habit of absorbing ultraviolet radiation.

The most likely explanations focus on fine particles, ice crystals, or even a chemical compound called iron chloride. Although it's much less likely, another possibility considered by scientists who study astrobiology is that these streaks could be made up of microbial life, Venus-style. Astrobiologists note that ring-shaped linkages of sulfur atoms, known to exist in Venus' atmosphere, could provide microbes with a kind of coating that would protect them from sulfuric acid. These handy chemical cloaks would also absorb potentially damaging ultraviolet light and re-radiate it as visible light.

Some of the Russian Venera probes did, indeed, detect particles in Venus' lower atmosphere about a micron in length – roughly the same size as a bacterium on Earth.

None of these findings provide compelling evidence for the existence of life in Venus' clouds. But the questions they raise, along with Venus' vanished ocean, its violently volcanic surface, and its hellish history, make a compelling case for a return to our temperamental sister planet. There is much, it would seem, that she can teach us.

Size and Distance

Our nearness to Venus is a matter of perspective. The planet is nearly as big around as Earth – 7,521 miles (12,104 kilometers) across, versus 7,926 miles (12,756 kilometers) for Earth. From Earth, Venus is the brightest object in the night sky after our own Moon. The ancients, therefore, gave it great importance in their cultures, even thinking it was two objects: a morning star and an evening star. That's where the trick of perspective comes in.

Because Venus' orbit is closer to the Sun than ours, the two of them – from our viewpoint – never stray far from each other. The ancient Egyptians and Greeks saw Venus in two guises: first in one orbital position (seen in the morning), then another (your "evening" Venus), just at different times of the year.

At its nearest to Earth, Venus is some 38 million miles (about 61 million kilometers) distant. But most of the time the two planets are farther apart; Mercury, the innermost planet, actually spends more time in Earth's proximity than Venus.

One more trick of perspective: how Venus looks through binoculars or a telescope. Keep watch over many months, and you'll notice that Venus has phases, just like our Moon – full, half, quarter, etc. The complete cycle, however, new to full, takes 584 days, while our Moon takes just a month. And it was this perspective, the phases of Venus first observed by Galileo through his telescope, that provided the key scientific proof for the Copernican heliocentric nature of the Solar System.

Orbit and Rotation

Spending a day on Venus would be quite a disorienting experience – that is, if your ship or suit could protect you from temperatures in the range of 900 degrees Fahrenheit (475 Celsius). For one thing, your "day" would be 243 Earth days long – longer even than a Venus year (one trip around the Sun), which takes only 225 Earth days. For another, because of the planet's extremely slow rotation, sunrise to sunset would take 117 Earth days. And by the way, the Sun would rise in the west and set in the east, because Venus spins backward compared to Earth.

While you're waiting, don't expect any seasonal relief from the unrelenting temperatures. On Earth, with its spin axis tilted by about 23 degrees, we experience summer when our part of the planet (our hemisphere) receives the Sun's rays more directly – a result of that tilt. In winter, the tilt means the rays are less direct. No such luck on Venus: Its very slight tilt is only three degrees, which is too little to produce noticeable seasons.

Moons

Venus has no moons.

Rings

Venus has no rings.

Formation

A critical question for scientists who search for life among the stars: How do habitable planets get their start? The close similarities of early Venus and Earth, and their very different fates, provide a kind of test case for scientists who study planet formation. Similar size, similar interior structure, both harboring oceans in their younger days. Yet one is now an inferno, while the other is the only known world – so far – to play host to abundant life. The factors that set these planets on almost opposite paths began, most likely, in the swirling disk of gas and dust from which they were born. Somehow, 4.6 billion years ago that disk around our Sun accreted, cooled, and settled into the planets we know today. Several might well have moved in closer, or farther out, as the solar system formed. Better knowledge of the formation history of Venus could help us better understand Earth's – and those of rocky planets around other stars.

Structure

If we could slice Venus and Earth in half, pole to pole, and place them side by side, they would look remarkably similar. Each planet has an iron core enveloped by a hot-rock mantle; the thinnest of skins forms a rocky, exterior crust. On both planets, this thin skin changes form and sometimes erupts into volcanoes in response to the ebb and flow of heat and pressure deep beneath.

Other possible similarities will require further investigation – and perhaps another visit to a planet that has hosted many Earth probes, both in orbit and (briefly) on the surface. On Earth, the slow movement of continents over thousands and millions of years reshapes the surface, a process known as "plate tectonics." Something similar might have happened on Venus early in its history. Today a key element of this process could be operating: subduction, or the sliding of one continental "plate" beneath another, which can also trigger volcanoes. Subduction is believed to be the first step in creating plate tectonics.

NASA's Magellan spacecraft, which ended a five-year mission to Venus in 1994, mapped the broiling surface using radar.

Magellan saw a land of extreme volcanism. The orbiter saw a relatively young surface, one recently reshaped (in geologic terms), and chains of towering mountains.

Surface

The broiling surface of Venus has been a topic of heated discussion among planetary scientists. The traditional picture includes a catastrophic, planetwide resurfacing between 350 and 750 million years ago. In other words, Venus appears to have completely erased most traces of its early surface. The causes: volcanic and tectonic forces, which could include surface buckling and massive eruptions. But newer estimates made with help from computer models paint a different portrait. While the same forces would be at work, resurfacing would be piecemeal over an extended time. The average age of surface features could be as young as 150 million years, with some older surfaces mixed in. Venus is a landscape of valleys and high mountains dotted with thousands of volcanoes. Its surface features - most named for both real and mythical women - include Ishtar Terra, a rocky, highland area around the size of Australia near the north pole, and an even larger, South-America-sized region called Aphrodite Terra that stretches across the equator. One mountain reaches 36,000 feet (11 kilometers), higher than Mt. Everest. Notably, except for Earth, Venus has by far the fewest impact craters of any rocky planet, revealing a young surface.

On your tour of Venus, during the 117 days you're waiting for sunset, you might stop by a volcanic crater, Sacajawea, named for Lewis and Clark's Native American guide. Or stroll through a deep canyon, Diana, named for the Roman goddess of the hunt.

Other notable features of the Venus landscape include:

"Pancake" domes with flat tops and steep sides, as wide as 38 miles (62 kilometers), likely formed by the extrusion of highly viscous lava.

"Tick" domes, odd volcanoes with radiating spurs that, from above, make them look like their blood-feeding namesake.

Tesserae, terrain with intricate patterns of ridges and grooves that suggest the scorching temperatures make rock behave in some ways more like peanut butter beneath a thin and strong chocolate layer on Venus.

Atmosphere

The Soviet Union landed 10 probes on the surface of Venus, but even among the few that functioned after landing, the successes were short-lived – the longest survivor lasted two hours; the shortest, 23 minutes. Photos snapped before the landers fried show a barren, dim, and rocky landscape, and a sky that is likely some shade of sulfur yellow.

Venus' atmosphere is one of extremes. With the hottest surface in the solar system, apart from the Sun itself, Venus is hotter even than the innermost planet, charbroiled Mercury. To outlive the short-lived Venera probes, your rambling sojourn on Venus would presumably include unimaginably strong insulation as temperatures push toward 900 degrees Fahrenheit (482 Celsius). You would need an extremely thick, pressurized outer shell to avoid being crushed by the weight of the atmosphere – which would press down on you as if you were 0.6 miles (1 kilometer) deep in the ocean.

The atmospheree is mostly carbon dioxide – the same gas driving the greenhouse effect on Venus and Earth – with clouds composed of sulfuric acid. And at the surface, the hot, high-pressure carbon dioxide behaves in a corrosive fashion. But a stranger transformation begins as you rise higher. Temperature and pressure begin to ease.

Magnetosphere

Even though Venus is similar in size to Earth and has a similar-sized iron core, the planet does not have its own internally generated magnetic field. Instead, Venus has what is known as an induced magnetic field. This weak magnetic field is created by the interaction of the Sun's magnetic field and the planet's outer atmosphere. Ultraviolet light from the Sun excites gases in Venus' outermost atmosphere; these electrically excited gases are called ions, and thus this region is called the ionosphere (Earth has an ionosphere as well). The solar wind – a million-mile-per-hour gale of electrically charged particles streaming continuously from the Sun – carries with it the Sun's magnetic field. When the Sun's magnetic field interacts with the electrically excited ionosphere of Venus, it creates or induces, a magnetic field there. This induced magnetic field envelops the planet and is shaped like an extended teardrop, or the tail of a comet, as the solar wind blows past Venus and outward into the solar system.

Chapter 4

The Earth

Overview

Our home planet is the third planet from the Sun, and the only place we know of so far that's inhabited by living things. The Moon Illusion: Why Does the Moon Look So Big Sometimes?

While Earth is only the fifth largest planet in the solar system, it is the only world in our solar system with liquid water on the surface. Just slightly larger than nearby Venus, Earth is the biggest of the four planets closest to the Sun, all of which are made of rock and metal.

The name Earth is at least 1,000 years old. All of the planets, except for Earth, were named after Greek and Roman gods and goddesses. However, the name Earth is a Germanic word, which simply means "the ground."

In Depth

Our home planet is the third planet from the Sun, and the only place we know of so far that's inhabited by living things. While Earth is only the fifth largest planet in the solar system, it is the only world in our solar system with liquid water on the surface. Just slightly larger than nearby Venus, Earth is the biggest of the four planets closest to the Sun, all of which are made of rock and metal.

Namesake

The name Earth is at least 1,000 years old. All of the planets, except for Earth, were named after Greek and Roman gods and goddesses. However, the name Earth is a Germanic word, which simply means "the ground."

Potential for Life

Earth has a very hospitable temperature and mix of chemicals that have made life abundant here. Most notably, Earth is unique in that most of our planet is covered in liquid water, since the temperature allows liquid water to exist for extended periods of time. Earth's vast oceans provided a convenient place for life to begin about 3.8 billion years ago.

Some of the features of our planet that make it great for sustaining life are changing due to the ongoing effects of climate change.

Size and Distance

With a radius of 3,959 miles (6,371 kilometers), Earth is the biggest of the terrestrial planets and the fifth largest planet overall.

From an average distance of 93 million miles (150 million kilometers), Earth is exactly one astronomical unit away from the Sun because one astronomical unit (abbreviated as AU), is the distance from the Sun to Earth. This unit provides an easy way to quickly compare planets' distances from the Sun.

It takes about eight minutes for light from the Sun to reach our planet.

Orbit and Rotation

As Earth orbits the Sun, it completes one rotation every 23.9 hours. It takes 365.25 days to complete one trip around the Sun. That extra quarter of a day presents a challenge to our calendar system, which counts one year as 365 days. To keep our yearly calendars consistent with our orbit around the Sun, every four years we add one day. That day is called a leap day, and the year it's added to is called a leap year.

Earth's axis of rotation is tilted 23.4 degrees with respect to the plane of Earth's orbit around the Sun. This tilt causes our yearly cycle of seasons. During part of the year, the northern hemisphere is tilted toward the Sun, and the southern hemisphere is tilted away. With the Sun higher in the sky, solar heating is greater in the north producing summer there. Less direct solar heating produces winter in the south. Six months later, the situation is reversed. When spring and fall begin, both hemispheres receive roughly equal amounts of heat from the Sun.

Moons

Earth is the only planet that has a single moon. Our Moon is the brightest and most familiar object in the night sky. In many ways, the Moon is responsible for making Earth such a great home. It stabilizes our planet's wobble, which has made the climate less variable over thousands of years.

Earth sometimes temporarily hosts orbiting asteroids or large rocks. They are typically trapped by Earth's gravity for a few months or years before returning to an orbit around the Sun.

Some asteroids will be in a long "dance" with Earth as both orbit the Sun.

Some moons are bits of rock that were captured by a planet's gravity, but our Moon is likely the result of a collision billions of years ago. When Earth was a young planet, a large chunk of rock smashed into it, displacing a portion of Earth's interior. The resulting chunks clumped together and formed our Moon. With a radius of 1,080 miles (1,738 kilometers), the Moon is the fifth largest moon in our solar system (after Ganymede, Titan, Callisto, and Io).

The Moon Is an average of 238,855 miles (384,400 kilometers) away from Earth. That means 30 Earth-sized planets could fit in between Earth and its Moon.

Rings

Earth has no rings.

Formation

When the solar system settled into its current layout about 4.5 billion years ago, Earth formed when gravity pulled swirling gas and dust in to become the third planet from the Sun. Like its fellow terrestrial planets, Earth has a central core, a rocky mantle, and a solid crust.

Structure

Earth is composed of four main layers, starting with an inner core at the planet's center, enveloped by the outer core, mantle, and crust.

The inner core is a solid sphere made of iron and nickel metals about 759 miles (1,221 kilometers) in radius. There the temperature is as high as 9,800 degrees Fahrenheit (5,400 degrees Celsius). Surrounding the inner core is the outer core. This layer is about 1,400 miles (2,300 kilometers) thick, made of iron and nickel fluids.

In between the outer core and crust is the mantle, the thickest layer. This hot, viscous mixture of molten rock is about 1,800 miles (2,900 kilometers) thick and has the consistency of caramel. The outermost layer, Earth's crust, goes about 19 miles (30 kilometers) deep on average on land. At the bottom of the ocean, the crust is thinner and extends about 3 miles (5 kilometers) from the seafloor to the top of the mantle.

Surface

Like Mars and Venus, Earth has volcanoes, mountains, and valleys. Earth's lithosphere, which includes the crust (both continental and oceanic) and the upper mantle, is divided into huge plates that are constantly moving. For example, the North American plate moves west over the Pacific Ocean basin, roughly at a rate equal to the growth of our fingernails. Earthquakes result when plates grind past one another, ride up over one another, collide to make mountains, or split and separate.

Earth's global ocean, which covers nearly 70% of the planet's surface, has an average depth of about 2.5 miles (4 kilometers) and contains 97% of Earth's water. Almost all of Earth's volcanoes are hidden under these oceans. Hawaii's Mauna Kea volcano is taller from base to summit than Mount Everest, but most of it is underwater. Earth's longest mountain range is also underwater, at the bottom of the Arctic and Atlantic oceans. It is four times longer than the Andes, Rockies and Himalayas combined.

Atmosphere

Near the surface, Earth has an atmosphere that consists of 78% nitrogen, 21% oxygen, and 1% other gases such as argon, carbon dioxide, and neon. The atmosphere affects Earth's long-term climate and short-term local weather and shields us from much of the harmful radiation coming from the Sun. It also protects us from meteoroids, most of which burn up in the atmosphere, seen as meteors in the night sky, before they can strike the surface as meteorites.

Magnetosphere

Our planet's rapid rotation and molten nickel-iron core give rise to a magnetic field, which the solar wind distorts into a teardrop shape in space. (The solar wind is a stream of charged particles continuously ejected from the Sun.) When charged particles from the solar wind become trapped in Earth's magnetic field, they collide with air molecules above our planet's magnetic poles. These air molecules then begin to glow and cause aurorae, or the northern and southern lights.

The magnetic field Is what causes compass needles to point to the North Pole regardless of which way you turn. But the magnetic polarity of Earth can change, flipping the direction of the magnetic field. The geologic record tells scientists that a magnetic reversal takes place about every 400,000 years on average, but the timing is very irregular. As far as we know, such a magnetic reversal doesn't cause any harm to life on

Earth, and a reversal is very unlikely to happen for at least another thousand years. But when it does happen, compass needles are likely to point in many different directions for a few centuries while the switch is being made. And after the switch is completed, they will all point south instead of north.

Chapter 5

The Mars

Overview

Mars is the fourth planet from the Sun – a dusty, cold, desert world with a very thin atmosphere. Mars is also a dynamic planet with seasons, polar ice caps, canyons, extinct volcanoes, and evidence that it was even more active in the past. NASA Retires InSight Mars Lander Mission After Years of Science

Mars is one of the most explored bodies in our solar system, and it's the only planet where we've sent rovers to roam the alien landscape.

NASA currently has two rovers (Curiosity and Perseverance), one lander (InSight), and one helicopter (Ingenuity) exploring the surface of Mars.

Perseverance rover – the largest, most advanced rover NASA has sent to another world – touched down on Mars on Feb. 18, 2021, after a 203-day journey traversing 293 million miles (472 million kilometers). The Ingenuity helicopter rode to Mars attached to the belly of Perseverance.

Perseverance is one of three spacecraft that arrived at Mars in 2021. The Hope orbiter from the United Arab Emirates arrived on Feb. 9, 2021. China's Tianwen-1 mission arrived on Feb. 10, 2021, and includes an orbiter, a lander, and a rover. Europe and India also have spacecraft studying Mars from orbit.

In May 2021, China became the second nation to ever land successfully on Mars when its Zhurong Mars rover touched down.

An International fleet of eight orbiters is studying the Red Planet from above including three NASA orbiters: 2001 Mars Odyssey, Mars Reconnaissance Orbiter, and MAVEN.

These robotic explorers have found lots of evidence that Mars was much wetter and warmer, with a thicker atmosphere, billions of years ago.

In Depth

Mars is no place for the faint-hearted. It's dry, rocky, and bitter cold. The fourth planet from the Sun, Mars is one of Earth's two closest planetary neighbors (Venus is the other). Mars is one of the easiest planets to spot in the night sky – it looks like a bright red point of light.

Despite being inhospitable to humans, robotic explorers – like NASA's new Perseverance rover – are serving as pathfinders to eventually get humans to the surface of the Red Planet.

Namesake

Mars was named by the ancient Romans for their god of war because its reddish color was reminiscent of blood. Other civilizations also named the planet for this attribute – for example, the Egyptians called it "Her Desher," meaning "the red one." Even today, it is frequently called the "Red Planet" because iron minerals in the Martian dirt oxidize, or rust, causing the surface to look red.

Potential for Life

Scientists don't expect to find living things currently thriving on Mars. Instead, they're looking for signs of life that existed long ago, when Mars was warmer and covered with water.

Size and Distance

With a radius of 2,106 miles (3,390 kilometers), Mars is about half the size of Earth. If Earth were the size of a nickel, Mars would be about as big as a raspberry.

From an average distance of 142 million miles (228 million kilometers), Mars is 1.5 astronomical units away from the Sun. One astronomical unit (abbreviated as AU), is the distance from the Sun to Earth. From this distance, it takes sunlight 13 minutes to travel from the Sun to Mars.

Orbit and Rotation

As Mars orbits the Sun, it completes one rotation every 24.6 hours, which is very similar to one day on Earth (23.9 hours). Martian days are called sols - short for "solar day." A year on Mars lasts 669.6 sols, which is the same as 687 Earth days.

Mars' axis of rotation is tilted 25 degrees with respect to the plane of its orbit around the Sun. This is another similarity with Earth, which has an axial tilt of 23.4 degrees. Like Earth, Mars has distinct seasons, but they last longer than seasons here on Earth since Mars takes longer to orbit the Sun (because it's farther away). And while here on Earth the seasons are evenly spread over the year, lasting 3 months (or one quarter of a year), on Mars the seasons vary in length because of Mars' elliptical, egg-shaped orbit around the Sun.

Spring in the northern hemisphere (autumn in the southern) is the longest season at 194 sols. Autumn in the northern hemisphere (spring in the southern) is the shortest at 142 days. Northern winter/southern summer is 154 sols, and northern summer/southern winter is 178 sols.

Moons

Mars has two small moons, Phobos and Deimos, that may be captured asteroids. They're potato-shaped because they have too little mass for gravity to make them spherical. The moons get their names from the horses that pulled the chariot of the Greek god of war, Ares.

Phobos, the innermost and larger moon, is heavily cratered, with deep grooves on its surface. It is slowly moving towards Mars and will crash into the planet or break apart in about 50 million years.

Deimos is about half as big as Phobos and orbits two and a half times farther away from Mars. Oddly-shaped Deimos is covered in loose dirt that often fills the craters on its surface, making it appear smoother than pockmarked Phobos.

Go farther. Explore the Moons of Mars ›

Rings

Mars has no rings. However, in 50 million years when Phobos crashes into Mars or breaks apart, it could create a dusty ring around the Red Planet.

Formation

When the solar system settled into its current layout about 4.5 billion years ago, Mars formed when gravity pulled swirling gas and dust in to become the fourth planet from the Sun. Mars is about half the size of Earth, and like its fellow terrestrial planets, it has a central core, a rocky mantle, and a solid crust.

Structure

Mars has a dense core at its center between 930 and 1,300 miles (1,500 to 2,100 kilometers) in radius. It's made of iron, nickel, and sulfur. Surrounding the core is a rocky mantle between 770 and 1,170 miles (1,240 to 1,880 kilometers) thick, and above that, a crust made of iron, magnesium, aluminum, calcium, and potassium. This crust is between 6 and 30 miles (10 to 50 kilometers) deep.

Surface

The Red Planet is actually many colors. At the surface, we see colors such as brown, gold, and tan. The reason Mars looks reddish is due to oxidization – or rusting – of iron in the rocks, regolith (Martian "soil"), and dust of Mars. This dust gets kicked up into the atmosphere and from a distance makes the planet appear mostly red.

Interestingly, while Mars is about half the diameter of Earth, its surface has nearly the same area as Earth's dry land. Its volcanoes, impact craters, crustal movement, and atmospheric conditions such as dust storms have altered the landscape of Mars over many years, creating some of the solar system's most interesting topographical features.

A large canyon system called Valles Marineris is long enough to stretch from California to New York – more than 3,000 miles (4,800 kilometers). This Martian canyon is 200 miles (320 kilometers) at its widest and 4.3 miles (7 kilometers) at its deepest. That's about 10 times the size of Earth's Grand Canyon.Mars is home to the largest volcano in the solar system, Olympus Mons. It's three times taller than Earth's Mt. Everest with a base the size of the state of New Mexico.

Mars appears to have had a watery past, with ancient river valley networks, deltas, and lakebeds, as well as rocks and minerals on the surface that could only have formed in liquid water. Some features suggest that Mars experienced huge floods about 3.5 billion years ago.

There is water on Mars today, but the Martian atmosphere is too thin for liquid water to exist for long on the surface. Today, water on Mars is found in the form of water-ice just under the surface in the polar regions as well as in briny (salty) water, which seasonally flows down some hillsides and crater walls.

Atmosphere

Mars has a thin atmosphere made up mostly of carbon dioxide, nitrogen, and argon gases. To our eyes, the sky would be hazy and red because of suspended dust instead of the familiar blue tint we see on Earth. Mars' sparse atmosphere doesn't offer much protection from impacts by such objects as meteorites, asteroids, and comets.

The temperature on Mars can be as high as 70 degrees Fahrenheit (20 degrees Celsius) or as low as about -225 degrees Fahrenheit (-153 degrees Celsius). And because the atmosphere is so thin, heat from the Sun easily escapes this planet. If you were to stand on the surface of Mars on the equator at noon, it would feel like spring at your feet (75 degrees Fahrenheit or 24 degrees Celsius) and winter at your head (32 degrees Fahrenheit or 0 degrees Celsius).

Occasionally, winds on Mars are strong enough to create dust storms that cover much of the planet. After such storms, it can be months before all of the dust settles.

Magnetosphere

Mars has no global magnetic field today, but areas of the Martian crust in the southern hemisphere are highly magnetized, indicating traces of a magnetic field from 4 billion years ago.

Chapter 6

The Jupiter

Overview

Jupiter has a long history of surprising scientists – all the way back to 1610 when Galileo Galilei found the first moons beyond Earth. That discovery changed the way we see the universe.Fifth in line from the Sun, Jupiter is, by far, the largest planet in the solar system – more than twice as massive as all the other planets combined.

Jupiter's familiar stripes and swirls are actually cold, windy clouds of ammonia and water, floating in an atmosphere of hydrogen and helium. Jupiter's iconic Great Red Spot is a giant storm bigger than Earth that has raged for hundreds of years.

One spacecraft – NASA's Juno orbiter – is currently exploring this giant world.

In Depth

Jupiter

Jupiter is the fifth planet from our Sun and is, by far, the largest planet in the solar system – more than twice as massive as all the other planets combined. Jupiter's stripes and swirls are actually cold, windy clouds of ammonia and water, floating in an atmosphere of hydrogen and helium. Jupiter's iconic

Great Red Spot is a giant storm bigger than Earth that has raged for hundreds of years.

Jupiter is surrounded by dozens of moons. Jupiter also has several rings, but unlike the famous rings of Saturn, Jupiter's rings are very faint and made of dust, not ice.

Namesake

Jupiter, being the biggest planet, gets its name from the king of the ancient Roman gods.

Potential for Life

Jupiter's environment is probably not conducive to life as we know it. The temperatures, pressures, and materials that characterize this planet are most likely too extreme and volatile for organisms to adapt to.

While planet Jupiter is an unlikely place for living things to take hold, the same is not true of some of its many moons. Europa is one of the likeliest places to find life elsewhere in our solar system. There is evidence of a vast ocean just beneath its icy crust, where life could possibly be supported.

Size and Distance

With a radius of 43,440.7 miles (69,911 kilometers), Jupiter is 11 times wider than Earth. If Earth were the size of a nickel, Jupiter would be about as big as a basketball.

From an average distance of 484 million miles (778 million kilometers), Jupiter is 5.2 astronomical units away from the Sun. One astronomical unit (abbreviated as AU), is the distance from the Sun to Earth. From this distance, it takes Sunlight 43 minutes to travel from the Sun to Jupiter.

Orbit and Rotation

Jupiter has the shortest day in the solar system. One day on Jupiter takes only about 10 hours (the time it takes for Jupiter to rotate or spin around once), and Jupiter makes a complete orbit around the Sun (a year in Jovian time) in about 12 Earth years (4,333 Earth days).

Its equator is tilted with respect to its orbital path around the Sun by just 3 degrees. This means Jupiter spins nearly upright and does not have seasons as extreme as other planets do.

Moons

With four large moons and many smaller moons, Jupiter forms a kind of miniature solar system. Jupiter has 80 moons. Fifty-seven moons have been given official names by the International Astronomical Union (IAU). Another 23 moons are awaiting names.

Jupiter's four largest moons - Io, Europa, Ganymede, and Callisto - were first observed by the astronomer Galileo Galilei in 1610 using an early version of the telescope. These four moons are known today as the Galilean satellites, and they're some of the most fascinating destinations in our solar system. Io is the most volcanically active body in the solar system. Ganymede is the largest moon in the solar system (even bigger than the planet Mercury). Callisto's very few small craters indicate a small degree of current surface activity. A liquid-water ocean with the ingredients for life may lie beneath the frozen crust of Europa, making it a tempting place to explore.

More on Jupiter's Moons

Rings

Discovered in 1979 by NASA's Voyager 1 spacecraft, Jupiter's rings were a surprise, as they are composed of small, dark particles and are difficult to see except when backlit by the Sun. Data from the Galileo spacecraft indicate that Jupiter's ring system may be formed by dust kicked up as interplanetary meteoroids smash into the giant planet's small innermost moons.

Formation

Jupiter took shape when the rest of the solar system formed about 4.5 billion years ago when gravity pulled swirling gas and dust in to become this gas giant. Jupiter took most of the mass left over after the formation of the Sun, ending up with more than twice the combined material of the other bodies in the solar system. In fact, Jupiter has the same ingredients as a star, but it did not grow massive enough to ignite.

About 4 billion years ago, Jupiter settled into its current position in the outer solar system, where it is the fifth planet from the Sun.

Structure

The composition of Jupiter is similar to that of the Sun - mostly hydrogen and helium. Deep in the atmosphere, pressure and temperature increase, compressing the hydrogen gas into a liquid. This gives Jupiter the largest ocean in the solar system – an ocean made of hydrogen instead of water. Scientists think that, at depths perhaps halfway to the planet's center, the pressure becomes so great that electrons are squeezed off the hydrogen atoms, making the liquid electrically conducting like metal. Jupiter's fast rotation is thought to drive electrical currents in this region, generating the planet's powerful magnetic field. It is still unclear if deeper down, Jupiter has a central core of solid material or if it may be a thick, super-hot and dense soup. It could be up to 90,032 degrees Fahrenheit (50,000 degrees Celsius) down there, made mostly of iron and silicate minerals (similar to quartz).

Surface

As a gas giant, Jupiter doesn't have a true surface. The planet is mostly swirling gases and liquids. While a spacecraft would have nowhere to land on Jupiter, it wouldn't be able to fly through unscathed either. The extreme pressures and temperatures deep inside the planet crush, melt, and vaporize spacecraft trying to fly into the planet.

Atmosphere

Jupiter's appearance is a tapestry of colorful cloud bands and spots. The gas planet likely has three distinct cloud layers in its "skies" that, taken together, span about 44 miles (71 kilometers). The top cloud is probably made of ammonia ice, while the middle layer is likely made of ammonium hydrosulfide crystals. The innermost layer may be made of water ice and vapor.

The vivid colors you see in thick bands across Jupiter may be plumes of sulfur and phosphorus-containing gases rising from the planet's warmer interior. Jupiter's fast rotation – spinning once every 10 hours – creates strong jet streams, separating its clouds into dark belts and bright zones across long stretches.

With no solid surface to slow them down, Jupiter's spots can persist for many years. Stormy Jupiter is swept by over a dozen prevailing winds, some reaching up to 335 miles per hour (539 kilometers per hour) at the equator. The Great Red Spot, a swirling oval of clouds twice as wide as Earth, has been observed on the giant planet for more than 300 years. More recently, three smaller ovals merged to form the Little Red Spot, about half the size of its larger cousin.

Findings from NASA's Juno probe released in October 2021 provide a fuller picture of what's going on below those clouds. Data from Juno shows that Jupiter's cyclones are warmer on top, with lower atmospheric densities, while they are colder at the bottom, with higher densities. Anticyclones, which rotate in the opposite direction, are colder at the top but warmer at the bottom.

The findings also Indicate these storms are far taller than expected, with some extending 60 miles (100 kilometers) below the cloud tops and others, including the Great Red Spot, extending over 200 miles (350 kilometers). This surprising discovery demonstrates that the vortices cover regions beyond those where water condenses and clouds form, below the depth where sunlight warms the atmosphere.

The height and size of the Great Red Spot mean the concentration of atmospheric mass within the storm potentially could be detectable by instruments studying Jupiter's gravity field. Two close Juno flybys over Jupiter's most famous spot provided the opportunity to search for the storm's gravity signature and complement the other results on its depth.

With their gravity data, the Juno team was able to constrain the extent of the Great Red Spot to a depth of about 300 miles (500 kilometers) below the cloud tops.

Belts and Zones In addition to cyclones and anticyclones, Jupiter is known for its distinctive belts and zones – white and reddish bands of clouds that wrap around the planet. Strong east-west winds moving in opposite directions separate the bands. Juno previously discovered that these winds, or jet streams, reach depths of about 2,000 miles (roughly 3,200 kilometers). Researchers are still trying to solve the mystery of how the jet streams form. Data collected by Juno during multiple passes reveal one possible clue: that the atmosphere's ammonia gas travels up and down in remarkable alignment with the observed jet streams.

Juno's data also shows that the belts and zones undergo a transition around 40 miles (65 kilometers) beneath Jupiter's water clouds. At shallow depths, Jupiter's belts are brighter in microwave light than the neighboring zones. But at deeper levels, below the water clouds, the opposite is true – which reveals a similarity to our oceans.

Polar Cyclones Juno previously discovered polygonal arrangements of giant cyclonic storms at both of Jupiter's poles – eight arranged in an octagonal pattern in the north and five arranged in a pentagonal pattern in the south. Over time, mission scientists determined these atmospheric phenomena are extremely resilient, remaining in the same location.

Juno data also indicates that, like hurricanes on Earth, these cyclones want to move poleward, but cyclones located at the center of each pole push them back. This balance explains where the cyclones reside and the different numbers at each pole.

Magnetosphere

The Jovian magnetosphere is the region of space influenced by Jupiter's powerful magnetic field. It balloons 600,000 to 2 million miles (1 to 3 million kilometers) toward the Sun (seven to 21 times the diameter of Jupiter itself) and tapers into a tadpole-shaped tail extending more than 600 million miles (1 billion kilometers) behind Jupiter, as far as Saturn's orbit. Jupiter's enormous magnetic field is 16 to 54 times as powerful as that of the Earth. It rotates with the planet and sweeps up particles that have an electric charge. Near the planet, the magnetic field traps swarms of charged particles and accelerates them to very high energies, creating intense radiation that bombards the innermost moons and can damage spacecraft.

Jupiter's magnetic field also causes some of the solar system's most spectacular aurorae at the planet's poles.

Chapter 7

The Saturn

Overview

Saturn is the sixth planet from the Sun and the second-largest planet in our solar system. Adorned with thousands of beautiful ringlets, Saturn is unique among the planets. It is not the only planet to have rings - made of chunks of ice and rock - but none are as spectacular or as complicated as Saturn's.

Like fellow gas giant Jupiter, Saturn is a massive ball made mostly of hydrogen and helium.

In Depth

Saturn is the sixth planet from the Sun and the second-largest planet in our solar system. Like fellow gas giant Jupiter, Saturn is a massive ball made mostly of hydrogen and helium. Saturn is not the only planet to have rings, but none are as spectacular or as complex as Saturn's. Saturn also has dozens of moons.

From the jets of water that spray from Saturn's moon Enceladus to the methane lakes on smoggy Titan, the Saturn system is a rich source of scientific discovery and still holds many mysteries.

Namesake

The farthest planet from Earth discovered by the unaided human eye, Saturn has been known since ancient times. The planet is named for the Roman god of agriculture and wealth, who was also the father of Jupiter.

Potential for Life

Saturn's environment is not conducive to life as we know it. The temperatures, pressures, and materials that characterize this planet are most likely too extreme and volatile for organisms to adapt to.

While planet Saturn is an unlikely place for living things to take hold, the same is not true of some of its many moons. Satellites like Enceladus and Titan, home to internal oceans, could possibly support life.

Size and Distance

With a radius of 36,183.7 miles (58,232 kilometers), Saturn is 9 times wider than Earth. If Earth were the size of a nickel, Saturn would be about as big as a volleyball.

From an average distance of 886 million miles (1.4 billion kilometers), Saturn is 9.5 astronomical units away from the Sun. One astronomical unit (abbreviated as AU), is the distance from the Sun to Earth. From this distance, it takes sunlight 80 minutes to travel from the Sun to Saturn.

Orbit and Rotation

Saturn has the second-shortest day in the solar system. One day on Saturn takes only 10.7 hours (the time it takes for Saturn to rotate or spin around once), and Saturn makes a complete orbit around the Sun (a year in Saturnian time) in about 29.4 Earth years (10,756 Earth days).

Its axis is tilted by 26.73 degrees with respect to its orbit around the Sun, which is similar to Earth's 23.5-degree tilt. This means that, like Earth, Saturn experiences seasons.

Moons

Saturn is home to a vast array of intriguing and unique worlds. From the haze-shrouded surface of Titan to crater-riddled Phoebe, each of Saturn's moons tells another piece of the story surrounding the Saturn system. Saturn has 83 moons. Sixty-three moons are confirmed and named, and another 20 moons are awaiting confirmation of discovery and official naming by the International Astronomical Union (IAU).

Rings

Saturn's rings are thought to be pieces of comets, asteroids, or shattered moons that broke up before they reached the planet, torn apart by Saturn's powerful gravity. They are made of billions of small chunks of ice and rock coated with other materials such as dust. The ring particles mostly range from tiny, dust-sized icy grains to chunks as big as a house. A few particles are as large as mountains. The rings would look mostly white if you looked at them from the cloud tops of

Saturn, and interestingly, each ring orbits at a different speed around the planet.

Saturn's ring system extends up to 175,000 miles (282,000 kilometers) from the planet, yet the vertical height is typically about 30 feet (10 meters) in the main rings. Named alphabetically in the order they were discovered, the rings are relatively close to each other, with the exception of a gap measuring 2,920 miles (4,700 kilometers) in width called the Cassini Division that separates Rings A and B. The main rings are A, B, and C. Rings D, E, F, and G are fainter and more recently discovered.

Starting at Saturn and moving outward, there is the D ring, C ring, B ring, Cassini Division, A ring, F ring, G ring, and finally, the E ring. Much farther out, there is the very faint Phoebe ring in the orbit of Saturn's moon Phoebe.

Formation

Saturn took shape when the rest of the solar system formed about 4.5 billion years ago when gravity pulled swirling gas and dust in to become this gas giant. About 4 billion years ago, Saturn settled into its current position in the outer solar system, where it is the sixth planet from the Sun. Like Jupiter, Saturn is mostly made of hydrogen and helium, the same two main components that make up the Sun.

Structure

Like Jupiter, Saturn is made mostly of hydrogen and helium. At Saturn's center is a dense core of metals like iron and nickel surrounded by rocky material and other compounds solidified by intense pressure and heat. It is enveloped by liquid metallic hydrogen inside a layer of liquid hydrogen – similar to Jupiter's core but considerably smaller.

It's hard to imagine, but Saturn is the only planet in our solar system with an average density that is less than water. The giant gas planet could float in a bathtub if such a colossal thing existed.

Surface

As a gas giant, Saturn doesn't have a true surface. The planet is mostly swirling gases and liquids deeper down. While a spacecraft would have nowhere to land on Saturn, it wouldn't be able to fly through unscathed either. The extreme pressures and temperatures deep inside the planet would crush, melt, and vaporize any spacecraft trying to fly into the planet.

Atmosphere

Saturn is blanketed with clouds that appear as faint stripes, jet streams, and storms. The planet is many different shades of yellow, brown, and gray.

Winds in the upper atmosphere reach 1,600 feet per second (500 meters per second) in the equatorial region. In contrast, the strongest hurricane-force winds on Earth top out at about 360 feet per second (110 meters per second). And the pressure – the same kind you feel when you dive deep underwater – is so powerful it squeezes gas into a liquid.

Saturn's north pole has an interesting atmospheric feature – a six-sided jet stream. This hexagon-shaped pattern was first noticed in images from the Voyager I spacecraft and has been more closely observed by the Cassini spacecraft since.

Spanning about 20,000 miles (30,000 kilometers) across, the hexagon is a wavy jet stream of 200-mile-per-hour winds (about 322 kilometers per hour) with a massive, rotating storm at the center. There is no weather feature like it anywhere else in the solar system.

Magnetosphere

Saturn's magnetic field is smaller than Jupiter's but still 578 times as powerful as Earth's. Saturn, the rings, and many of the satellites lie totally within Saturn's enormous magnetosphere, the region of space in which the behavior of electrically charged particles is influenced more by Saturn's magnetic field than by the solar wind.

Aurorae occur when charged particles spiral into a planet's atmosphere along magnetic field lines. On Earth, these charged particles come from the solar wind. Cassini showed that at least some of Saturn's aurorae are like Jupiter's and are largely unaffected by the solar wind. Instead, these aurorae are caused by a combination of particles ejected from Saturn's moons and Saturn's magnetic field's rapid rotation rate. But these "non-solar-originating" aurorae are not completely understood yet.

Chapter 8

The Uranus

Overview

Uranus is the seventh planet from the Sun, and has the third-largest diameter in our solar system. It was the first planet found with the aid of a telescope, Uranus was discovered in 1781 by astronomer William Herschel, although he originally thought it was either a comet or a star. It was two years later that the object was universally accepted as a new planet, in part because of observations by astronomer Johann Elert Bode. Herschel tried unsuccessfully to name his discovery Georgium Sidus after King George III. Instead, the scientific community accepted Bode's suggestion to name it Uranus, the Greek god of the sky, as suggested by Bode.

In Depth

The seventh planet from the Sun with the third largest diameter in our solar system, Uranus is very cold and windy. The ice giant is surrounded by 13 faint rings and 27 small moons as it rotates at a nearly 90-degree angle from the plane of its orbit. This unique tilt makes Uranus appear to spin sideways, orbiting the Sun like a rolling ball.

The first planet found with the aid of a telescope, Uranus was discovered in 1781 by astronomer William Herschel, although he originally thought it was either a comet or a star.

It was two years later that the object was universally accepted as a new planet, in part because of observations by astronomer Johann Elert Bode.

Namesake

William Herschel tried unsuccessfully to name his discovery Georgium Sidus after King George III. Instead, the planet was named for Uranus, the Greek god of the sky, as suggested by Johann Bode.

Potential for Life

Uranus' environment is not conducive to life as we know it. The temperatures, pressures, and materials that characterize this planet are most likely too extreme and volatile for organisms to adapt to.

Size and Distance

With a radius of 15,759.2 miles (25,362 kilometers), Uranus is 4 times wider than Earth. If Earth was the size of a nickel, Uranus would be about as big as a softball.

From an average distance of 1.8 billion miles (2.9 billion kilometers), Uranus is 19.8 astronomical units away from the Sun. One astronomical unit (abbreviated as AU), is the distance from the Sun to Earth. From this distance, it takes sunlight 2 hours and 40 minutes to travel from the Sun to Uranus.

Orbit and Rotation

One day on Uranus takes about 17 hours (the time it takes for Uranus to rotate or spin once). And Uranus makes a complete orbit around the Sun (a year in Uranian time) in about 84 Earth years (30,687 Earth days).

Uranus is the only planet whose equator is nearly at a right angle to its orbit, with a tilt of 97.77 degrees – possibly the result of a collision with an Earth-sized object long ago. This unique tilt causes the most extreme seasons in the solar system. For nearly a quarter of each Uranian year, the Sun shines directly over each pole, plunging the other half of the planet into a 21-year-long, dark winter.

Uranus is also one of just two planets that rotate in the opposite direction than most of the planets (Venus is the other one), from east to west.

Moons

Uranus has 27 known moons. While most of the satellites orbiting other planets take their names from Greek or Roman mythology, Uranus' moons are unique in being named for characters from the works of William Shakespeare and Alexander Pope.

All of Uranus' inner moons appear to be roughly half water ice and half rock. The composition of the outer moons remains unknown, but they are likely captured asteroids.

Rings

Uranus has two sets of rings. The inner system of nine rings consists mostly of narrow, dark grey rings. There are two outer rings: the innermost one is reddish like dusty rings elsewhere in the solar system, and the outer ring is blue like Saturn's E ring.

In order of increasing distance from the planet, the rings are called Zeta, 6, 5, 4, Alpha, Beta, Eta, Gamma, Delta, Lambda, Epsilon, Nu, and Mu. Some of the larger rings are surrounded by belts of fine dust.

Formation

Uranus took shape when the rest of the solar system formed about 4.5 billion years ago – when gravity pulled swirling gas and dust in to become this ice giant. Like its neighbor Neptune, Uranus likely formed closer to the Sun and moved to the outer solar system about 4 billion years ago, where it is the seventh planet from the Sun.

Structure

Uranus is one of two ice giants in the outer solar system (the other is Neptune). Most (80% or more) of the planet's mass is made up of a hot dense fluid of "icy" materials – water, methane, and ammonia – above a small rocky core. Near the core, it heats up to 9,000 degrees Fahrenheit (4,982 degrees Celsius).

Uranus is slightly larger in diameter than its neighbor Neptune, yet smaller in mass. It is the second least dense planet; Saturn is the least dense of all.

Uranus gets its blue-green color from methane gas in the atmosphere. Sunlight passes through the atmosphere and is reflected back out by Uranus' cloud tops. Methane gas absorbs the red portion of the light, resulting in a blue-green color.

Surface

As an ice giant, Uranus doesn't have a true surface. The planet is mostly swirling fluids. While a spacecraft would have nowhere to land on Uranus, it wouldn't be able to fly through its atmosphere unscathed either. The extreme pressures and temperatures would destroy a metal spacecraft.

Atmosphere

Uranus' atmosphere is mostly hydrogen and helium, with a small amount of methane and traces of water and ammonia. The methane gives Uranus its signature blue color.

While Voyager 2 saw only a few discrete clouds, a Great Dark Spot, and a small dark spot during its flyby in 1986 – more recent observations reveal that Uranus exhibits dynamic clouds as it approaches equinox, including rapidly changing bright features.

Uranus' planetary atmosphere, with a minimum temperature of 49K (-224.2 degrees Celsius) makes it even colder than Neptune in some places.

Wind speeds can reach up to 560 miles per hour (900 kilometers per hour) on Uranus. Winds are retrograde at the equator, blowing in the reverse direction of the planet's rotation. But closer to the poles, winds shift to a prograde direction, flowing with Uranus' rotation.

Magnetosphere

Uranus has an unusual, irregularly shaped magnetosphere. Magnetic fields are typically in alignment with a planet's rotation, but Uranus' magnetic field is tipped over: the magnetic axis is tilted nearly 60 degrees from the planet's axis of rotation, and is also offset from the center of the planet by one-third of the planet's radius.

Auroras on Uranus are not in line with the poles (like they are on Earth, Jupiter, and Saturn) due to the lopsided magnetic field.

The magnetosphere tail behind Uranus opposite the Sun extends into space for millions of miles. Its magnetic field lines are twisted by Uranus' sideways rotation into a long corkscrew shape.

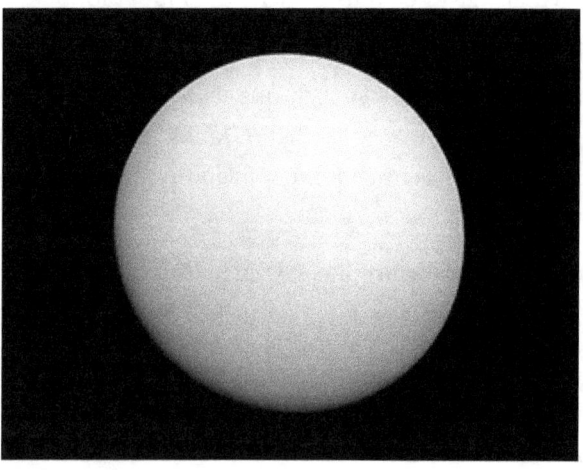

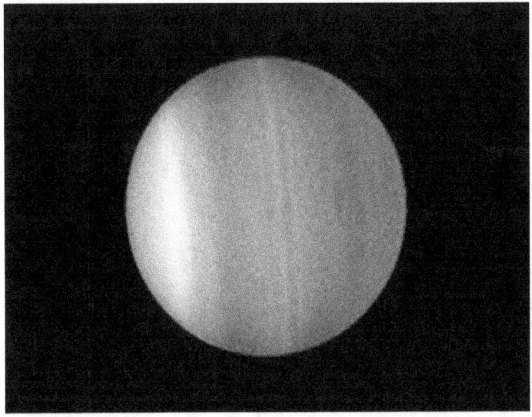

Hubble Uranus

Rings Of Uranus

Chapter 9

The Neptune

Overview

Dark, cold, and whipped by supersonic winds, ice giant Neptune is the eighth and most distant planet in our solar system.More than 30 times as far from the Sun as Earth, Neptune is the only planet in our solar system not visible to the naked eye and the first predicted by mathematics before its discovery. In 2011 Neptune completed its first 165-year orbit since its discovery in 1846.

NASA's Voyager 2 is the only spacecraft to have visited Neptune up close. It flew past in 1989 on its way out of the solar system.

In Depth

Dark, cold, and whipped by supersonic winds, ice giant Neptune is the eighth and most distant planet in our solar system. More than 30 times as far from the Sun as Earth, Neptune is the only planet in our solar system not visible to the naked eye. In 2011 Neptune completed its first 165-year orbit since its discovery in 1846.

Neptune is so far from the Sun that high noon on the big blue planet would seem like dim twilight to us. The warm light we see here on our home planet is roughly 900 times as bright as sunlight on Neptune.

Namesake

The ice giant Neptune was the first planet located through mathematical calculations. Using predictions made by Urbain Le Verrier, Johann Galle discovered the planet in 1846. The planet is named after the Roman god of the sea, as suggested by Le Verrier.

Potential for Life

Neptune's environment is not conducive to life as we know it. The temperatures, pressures, and materials that characterize this planet are most likely too extreme and volatile for organisms to adapt to.

Size and Distance

With a radius of 15,299.4 miles (24,622 kilometers), Neptune is about four times wider than Earth. If Earth were the size of a nickel, Neptune would be about as big as a baseball.

From an average distance of 2.8 billion miles (4.5 billion kilometers), Neptune is 30 astronomical units away from the Sun. One astronomical unit (abbreviated as AU), is the distance from the Sun to Earth. From this distance, it takes sunlight 4 hours to travel from the Sun to Neptune.

Orbit and Rotation

One day on Neptune takes about 16 hours (the time it takes for Neptune to rotate or spin once). And Neptune makes a complete orbit around the Sun (a year in Neptunian time) in about 165 Earth years (60,190 Earth days).

Sometimes Neptune is even farther from the Sun than dwarf planet Pluto. Pluto's highly eccentric, oval-shaped orbit brings it inside Neptune's orbit for a 20-year period every 248 Earth years. This switch, in which Pluto is closer to the Sun than Neptune, happened most recently from 1979 to 1999. Pluto can never crash into Neptune, though, because for every three laps Neptune takes around the Sun, Pluto makes two. This repeating pattern prevents close approaches of the two bodies.

Neptune's axis of rotation is tilted 28 degrees with respect to the plane of its orbit around the Sun, which is similar to the axial tilts of Mars and Earth. This means that Neptune experiences seasons just like we do on Earth; however, since its year is so long, each of the four seasons lasts for over 40 years.

Moons

Neptune has 14 known moons. Neptune's largest moon Triton was discovered on October 10, 1846, by William Lassell, just 17 days after Johann Gottfried Galle discovered the planet. Since Neptune was named for the Roman god of the sea, its moons are named for various lesser sea gods and nymphs in Greek mythology.

Triton is the only large moon in the solar system that circles its planet in a direction opposite to the planet's rotation (a retrograde orbit), which suggests that it may once have been an independent object that Neptune captured. Triton is extremely cold, with surface temperatures around minus 391 degrees Fahrenheit (minus 235 degrees Celsius). And yet, despite this deep freeze at Triton, Voyager 2 discovered geysers spewing icy material upward more than 5 miles (8 kilometers).

Triton's thin atmosphere, also discovered by Voyager, has been detected from Earth several times since, and is growing warmer, but scientists do not yet know why.

Solar System ExplorationOur Galactic NeighborhoodSkip Navigation

Neptune

NEPTUNE

MENU

ON THIS PAGE

Dark, cold, and whipped by supersonic winds, ice giant Neptune is the eighth and most distant planet in our solar system. More than 30 times as far from the Sun as Earth, Neptune is the only planet in our solar system not visible to the naked eye. In 2011 Neptune completed its first 165-year orbit since its discovery in 1846.

Neptune is so far from the Sun that high noon on the big blue planet would seem like dim twilight to us. The warm light we see here on our home planet is roughly 900 times as bright as sunlight on Neptune.

Namesake

The ice giant Neptune was the first planet located through mathematical calculations. Using predictions made by Urbain Le Verrier, Johann Galle discovered the planet in 1846. The planet is named after the Roman god of the sea, as suggested by Le Verrier.

Potential for Life

Neptune's environment is not conducive to life as we know it. The temperatures, pressures, and materials that characterize this planet are most likely too extreme and volatile for organisms to adapt to.

Size and Distance

With a radius of 15,299.4 miles (24,622 kilometers), Neptune is about four times wider than Earth. If Earth were the size of a nickel, Neptune would be about as big as a baseball.

From an average distance of 2.8 billion miles (4.5 billion kilometers), Neptune is 30 astronomical units away from the Sun. One astronomical unit (abbreviated as AU), is the distance from the Sun to Earth. From this distance, it takes sunlight 4 hours to travel from the Sun to NEPTUNE

Orbit and Rotation

One day on Neptune takes about 16 hours (the time it takes for Neptune to rotate or spin once). And Neptune makes a complete orbit around the Sun (a year in Neptunian time) in about 165 Earth years (60,190 Earth days).

Sometimes Neptune is even farther from the Sun than dwarf planet Pluto. Pluto's highly eccentric, oval-shaped orbit brings it inside Neptune's orbit for a 20-year period every 248 Earth years. This switch, in which Pluto is closer to the Sun than Neptune, happened most recently from 1979 to 1999. Pluto can never crash into Neptune, though, because for every three laps Neptune takes around the Sun, Pluto makes two. This repeating pattern prevents close approaches of the two bodies.

Neptune's axis of rotation is tilted 28 degrees with respect to the plane of its orbit around the Sun, which is similar to the axial tilts of Mars and Earth. This means that Neptune experiences seasons just like we do on Earth; however, since its year is so long, each of the four seasons lasts for over 40 years.

Moons

Neptune has 14 known moons. Neptune's largest moon Triton was discovered on October 10, 1846, by William Lassell, just 17 days after Johann Gottfried Galle discovered the planet. Since Neptune was named for the Roman god of the sea, its moons are named for various lesser sea gods and nymphs in Greek mythology.

Triton is the only large moon in the solar system that circles its planet in a direction opposite to the planet's rotation (a retrograde orbit), which suggests that it may once have been an independent object that Neptune captured. Triton is extremely cold, with surface temperatures around minus 391 degrees Fahrenheit (minus 235 degrees Celsius). And yet, despite this deep freeze at Triton, Voyager 2 discovered geysers spewing icy material upward more than 5 miles (8 kilometers). Triton's thin atmosphere, also discovered by Voyager, has been detected from Earth several times since, and is growing warmer, but scientists do not yet know why.

Rings

Fuzzy image of Neptune's rings.

This Voyager 2 image, taken in 1989, was the first to show Neptune's rings in detail. Credit: NASA/JPL

Neptune has at least five main rings and four prominent ring arcs that we know of so far. Starting near the planet and moving outward, the main rings are named Galle, Leverrier, Lassell, Arago, and Adams. The rings are thought to be relatively young and short-lived.

Neptune's ring system also has peculiar clumps of dust called arcs. Four prominent arcs named Liberté (Liberty), Egalité (Equality), Fraternité (Fraternity), and Courage are in the outermost ring, Adams. The arcs are strange because the laws of motion would predict that they would spread out evenly rather than stay clumped together. Scientists now think the gravitational effects of Galatea, a moon just inward from the ring, stabilizes these arcs.

Formation

Neptune took shape when the rest of the solar system formed about 4.5 billion years ago when gravity pulled swirling gas and dust in to become this ice giant. Like its neighbor Uranus, Neptune likely formed closer to the Sun and moved to the outer solar system about 4 billion years ago.

Structure

Neptune is one of two ice giants in the outer solar system (the other is Uranus). Most (80% or more) of the planet's mass is made up of a hot dense fluid of "icy" materials - water, methane, and ammonia - above a small, rocky core. Of the giant planets, Neptune is the densest.

Scientists think there might be an ocean of super hot water under Neptune's cold clouds. It does not boil away because incredibly high pressure keeps it locked inside.

Surface

Neptune does not have a solid surface. Its atmosphere (made up mostly of hydrogen, helium, and methane) extends to great depths, gradually merging into water and other melted ices over a heavier, solid core with about the same mass as Earth.

Atmosphere

Neptune's atmosphere is made up mostly of hydrogen and helium with just a little bit of methane. Neptune's neighbor Uranus is a blue-green color due to such atmospheric methane, but Neptune is a more vivid, brighter blue, so there must be an unknown component that causes the more intense color.

Neptune is our solar system's windiest world. Despite its great distance and low energy input from the Sun, Neptune's winds can be three times stronger than Jupiter's and nine times stronger than Earth's. These winds whip clouds of frozen methane across the planet at speeds of more than 1,200 miles per hour (2,000 kilometers per hour). Even Earth's most powerful winds hit only about 250 miles per hour (400 kilometers per hour).

In 1989 a large, oval-shaped storm in Neptune's southern hemisphere dubbed the "Great Dark Spot" was large enough to contain the entire Earth. That storm has since disappeared, but new ones have appeared on different parts of the planet.

Magnetosphere

The main axis of Neptune's magnetic field is tipped over by about 47 degrees compared with the planet's rotation axis. Like Uranus, whose magnetic axis is tilted about 60 degrees from the axis of rotation, Neptune's magnetosphere undergoes wild variations during each rotation because of this misalignment. The magnetic field of Neptune is about 27 times more powerful than that of Earth.

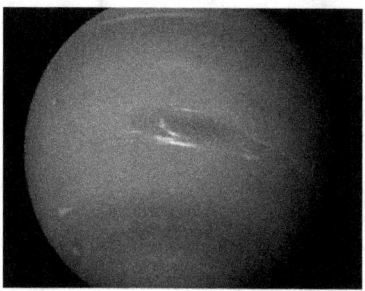

Neptune

Neptune Rings

www.ingramcontent.com/pod-product-compliance
Lightning Source LLC
LaVergne TN
LVHW010605070526
838199LV00063BA/5081